Robert Gamble

Orderly Book of Captain Robert Gamble

of the Second Virginia Regiment

Robert Gamble

Orderly Book of Captain Robert Gamble
of the Second Virginia Regiment

ISBN/EAN: 9783337091781

Printed in Europe, USA, Canada, Australia, Japan

Cover: Foto ©Andreas Hilbeck / pixelio.de

More available books at **www.hansebooks.com**

INTRODUCTION.

The original of the fragment of the Orderly Book of Captain Robert Gamble, herewith published, was presented to the Virginia Historical Society by Hon. Joseph Addison Waddell, Staunton, Virginia, some years ago. Mr. Waddell obtained it from William H. Gamble, Esq., a descendant of Captain Gamble, and gave some extracts from it in his "Annals of Augusta County, Virginia," to which valuable work the editor acknowledges his indebtedness.

The grandfather of Captain Gamble (also named Robert) was a native of Londonderry, Ireland (in the famous seige of which in 1689, a Gamble is said to have lost his life), and was an immigrant to Augusta county, Virginia, about the year 1735. He brought with him his wife and a son, James, born in 1729. Mr. Waddell mentions another son, Joseph, who, he states, was probably the ancestor of the Gambles of Ohio and Missouri. James Gamble had issue two sons, Robert and John, and three daughters, Agnes, Elizabeth and Esther, who married, severally, Davis, Moffett and Bell.

Robert, the elder son, was born September 3, 1754, and was educated at Liberty Hall Academy, the initial of the admirable Washington-Lee University. He is stated to have entered the service of the Revolution as first lieutenant of the first company raised in Augusta county. He soon succeeded to the command of the company. He was in active service during the entire period of the war and participated in many battles, including those of Princeton and Monmouth. It is claimed by his descendants that he led a pioneer assault in the storming of Stony Point. This memorable event has been peculiarly impressed on the imagination of the goodly people of Richmond, in that the historic and socially excellent metropolis was favored in the worthy citizenship of two invincible leaders in the reduction of Stony Point, Captain Robert Gamble and Major James Gibbon.[1]

Lossing gives the following account of the memorable achieve-ment: "On the morning of the 15th of July, 1779, all the Massachusetts light infantry were marched to the quarters of Wayne at Sandy Beach, fourteen miles from Stony Point. At meridian on that exceedingly sultry day, the whole body moved through narrow defiles, over rough crags and across deep morasses in single file, and at eight in the evening rendezvoused a mile and a half below Stony Point. There they remained until General Wayne and several officers returned from recon-noitreing the works of the enemy, when they were formed into column, and moved silently forward under the guidance of a negro slave belonging to a Captain Lamb, who resided in the neighborhood. The position of the fortress was such that it seemed almost impregnable. Situated upon a huge rocky bluff, an island at high water, and always inaccessible dry-shod, except across a narrow causeway in the rear, it was strongly defended by outworks and a double row of *abatis*. Upon three sides of the rock were the waters of the Hudson, and on the fourth was a morass, deep and dangerous. But Wayne was not easily deterred by obstacles; and tradition avers that while conversing with Washington on the subject of this expedition, he remarked with emphasis: "General, I'll storm hell if *you* will only plan it." He possessed the true fire of the flint, and was always governed by the maxim, "Where there's a will there's a way."

[1] Then Lieutenant Gibbon, of the Sixth Pennsylvania Infantry, and subsequently promoted major. He was appointed collector of the Port of Richmond in 1802. Having been admitted a member of the New York Society of the Cincinnati, he transferred his membership to the Virginia Society, of which he was the last treasurer. He died July 1, 1834, in the seventy-seventh year of his age, and is buried in Shockoe Hill Cemetery at Richmond. A son, Lieutenant James Gibbon, United States Navy, lost his life in the burning of the Richmond Theatre, De-cember 26, 1811. Rev. Charles Minnegerode, D. D., so long the beloved rector of St. Paul's Church, married a granddaughter of Major James Gibbon. A fine portrait of him, by John B. Martin, is among the pictures owned by the Virginia Historical Society.

He resolved to storm the fort at all hazards, and only waited for the ebbing of the tide and the deep first slumber of the garrison to move toward the fortress.   It was half past eleven o'clock at night when the Americans commenced their silent march toward the fort.   All the dogs in the neighborhood had been killed the day before, that their barking might not give notice of strangers near.   The negro, with two strong men disguised as farmers, advanced alone.   The countersign was given to the first sentinel on the high ground west of the morass, and while he was conversing with Pompey, the men seized and gagged him.   The silence of the sentinel at the causeway was secured in the same manner, and as soon as the tide ebbed sufficiently, the whole of Wayne's little army, except a detachment of three hundred men under General Muhlenburg, who remained in the rear as a reserve, crossed the morass to the foot of the western declivity of the promonotory, unobserved by the enemy.   The troops were now divided into two columns; the van of the right, consisting of one hundred and fifty volunteers, under Lieutenant-Colonel De Fleury,[2] and that of the left, of one hundred volunteers under Major Stewart, each with unloaded muskets and fixed bayonets.   An *avant-guard* of twenty picked men for each company, under Lieutenants Gibbon and Knox, preceded them to remove the *abatis* and other obstructions.   These vans composed the forlorn hope on that memorable night.   At a little past midnight the advanced parties moved silently to the charge, one company on the southern and the other on the northern portion of the height.

They were followed by the two main divisions ; the right composed of the regiments of Febiger and Meigs, being led by General Wayne in person.   The left was composed of Colonel

---

[2] Louis de Fleury, a descendant of Hercule Andre de Fleury, a French nobleman, who was the preceptor of the grandson of Louis XIV.   He was afterwards made Cardinal and Prime Minister.   De Fleury came to America early in the Revolution ; was received kindly by Washington, who gave him a commission.   Educated as an engineer, his talents were soon brought into requisition.   He acted in that capacity at Fort Mifflin.   For his gallantry at the battle of Brandywine Congress voted him a horse.   He returned to France soon after the capture of Stony Point.

Butler's[3] regiment and two companies under Major Murfey.[4] The Americans were undiscovered until within pistol shot of the pickets upon the heights, when a skirmish ensued between the sentinels and the advance guards. The pickets fired several shots, but the Americans, true to orders, relied entirely on the bayonet, and pressed forward with vigor. The garrison was aroused from their slumbers, and instantly the deep silence of the night was broken by the roll of the drum, the loud cry of *To Arms! To Arms!* the rattle of musketry from the ramparts and behind the *abatis*, and the roar of cannon charged with deadly grape-shot from the embrasures. In the face of this terrible storm the Americans forced their way, at the point of the bayonet, through every obstacle, until the van of each column met in the centre of the works, where each arrived at the same time.[5] At the inner *abatis* Wayne was struck upon the head by a musket ball, which brought him upon his knees. His two brave aids, Fishburne and Archer raised him to his feet, and carried him gallantly through the works.[6]

Believing himself mortally wounded, the General exclaimed as he arose, "March on! carry me into the front, for I will die

[3] Richard Butler was appointed major of the Eighth Pennsylvania regiment July 20, 1776; promoted lieutenant-colonel March 12, 1777; transferred as lieutenant-colonel of Morgan's Riflemen June 9, 1777; is promoted colonel of the Ninth Pennsylvania, dating from June 7, 1777; by an alteration subsequent to March 12, 1777, he was transferred to the command of the Seventeenth Pennsylvania, January 1, 1783, he was in command of the Third Pennsylvania. He was second in command under General Arthur St. Clair in his ill-fated expedition, and was killed in the battle of November 4, 1791, which terminated in the defeat of St. Claire's army. (*Pennsylvania in the Revolution.* Edited by John Blair Lynn and William H. Egle, M. D. Vol. I.) The editor is further indebted to this valuable work.

[4] It will be found that a Major Murfey is mentioned in the Orderly Book of date August 21, 1779, and subsequently, but the editor has been unable to identify him with any special command. Watson, in his *Annals of New York* (p. 65), mentions "the celebrated Murphy, a man who had belonged to Morgan's Rifle Corps."

[5] Major (afterwards General) Hall states in his memoir: "Each of our men had a white paper in his hat, which in the darkness distinguished him from the enemy; and the watch-word was '*The fort's our own.*'"

[6] Wayne's official dispatch, dated Stony Point, July 17, 1779.

at the head of my column!'' But the wound was not very severe, and he was able to join in the loud huzzas that arose when the two columns met as victors within the fort. Colonel De Fleury first entered the works, and struck the British standard with his own hands.[1] The garrison surrendered at discretion as prisoners of war, and that brilliant achievement was rendered the more glorious for the clemency which the victors exercised toward the vanquished. Not a life was taken after the flag was struck and the garrison had pleaded for quarters. Wayne had but fifteen killed and eighty-three wounded; the British had sixty-three killed, and Johnson, the commander, with five hundred and forty-three officers and men were made prisoners. The ships of the enemy, lying in the river in front of Stony Point, slipped their cables and moved down to a place of security. Before daylight, ' Mad Anthony' sent to the commander-in-chief this brief and comprehensive reply :

STONY POINT, *16th July, 1779.*
2 o'clock A. M.
DEAR GENERAL :

The fort and garrison, with Colonel Johnston, are ours. Our officers and men behaved like men who are determined to be free.   Yours most sincerely,

ANT'Y WAYNE.
General Washington.

At dawn the next morning the cannons of the captured fort were turned upon the enemy's works at Verplanck's Point, under Colonel Webster, and a desultory bombardment was kept up during the day. Major-General Robert Howe had been sent to attack Fort Fayette, but on account of delays and

[1] Waddell states that Captain Gamble led one of the assailing parties, and that " he with his men mounted the wall in immediate vicinity of a cannon, and seeing the match about to be applied, barely had time to lower his head and order his men to fall flat before the gun was discharged. He was, however, permanently deafened by the concussion. His company immediately moved on, and were the first to enter the fort. Being busily engaged in securing prisoners, the British flag was overlooked until Lieutenant-Colonel De Fleury observed it and pulled it down. At this stage the Pennsylvania troops entered the fort "—*Annals of Augusta County, Virginia*, p. 188.

some misconception of Washington's orders, he did not make the attack in time to dislodge the garrison.

News of Webster's critical situation and the capture of Stony Point was speedily communicated to Sir Henry Clinton, and he immediately sent relief to the menaced garrison at Verplanck's. Howe withdrew, and the enterprise was abandoned.

The British repossessed themselves of Stony Point on the 20th, but they had little of value left them but the eligible site for a fortification. The storming and capture of Stony Point, regarded as an exhibition of skill and indomitable courage, was one of the most brilliant events of the war. General Wayne, the leader of the enterprise, was everywhere greeted with raptuous applause. Congress testified their grateful sense of his services by a vote of thanks ' for his brave, prudent and soldiery conduct.' It was also resolved that a medal of gold, emblematic of this action, should be struck and presented to General Wayne. Thanks were also presented by Congress to Lieutenant-Colonel De Fleury and Major John Stewart, and a medal of silver was ordered to be struck and presented to each.

The conduct of Lieutenants Gibbon [8] and Knox [9] was warmly applauded, and brevets of Captain were given to each, and to Mr. Archer, the volunteer aid of Wayne, who was the bearer of the General's letter to Washington on the occasion. Pursuant to the recommendation of the commander-in-chief, and in fulfilment of promises made by Wayne before the assault, with the concurrence of Washington, Congress resolved, ' That the value of the military stores taken at Stony Point be ascertained and divided among the gallant troops by whom it was reduced, in such manner and proportions as the commander-in-chief shall prescribe.' [10]

From the following, which is labelled " Captain Gamble's Company, Prize Roll for Stony Point," it would appear that the company commanded by him on the occasion was composed of volunteers. [11]

[8] Lieutenant Gibbon lost seventeen men, killed and wounded, in the attack.

[9] George Knox, of the Ninth Pennsylvania regiment.

[10] *Field Book of the Revolution*, Vol. II, pp. 744, 750.

[11] Furnished by Dr. Cary B. Gamble, Baltimore Md.

A Return of the Men of Captain Gamble's Company when Stony Point was taken from the Enemy, 15th July, 1779.

Robert Gamble, Captain.
David Williams, Lieutenant.
William Spencer, Sergeant Eighth Volunteer Regiment.
George Grimes, Sergeant First State Volunteer Reg't.
Richard Piles, Sergeant Eighth Volunteer Regiment.
Randolph Death, Corporal Eighth Volunteer Regiment.
Samuel Glen, Corporal Seventh Volunteer Regiment.
Jesse Page, Corporal Eighth Volunteer Regiment.
John Farrell, Drummer Seventh Volunteer Regiment.

Belonging to the Seventh Virginia Regiment:

Joshua Haycraft,	William Gibbs.
Mathias Martin,	William Hinds,
Alexander Dresdal,	Daniel Rich,
John Malvin,	Aaron Redmond,
Peter Sherriden,	Thomas Miller,
Joseph Fox,	William Campbell,
Daniel Burcher,	Moses Plain,
Thomas Roberts,	Peter Barret,
Sylvester Hurly,	Alexander Strickling.

Charles Steward.

Belonging to the Eighth Virginia Regiment:

George Ward,	Michael Moore,
John Bray,	James L. Masters,
James Balls,	Richard Barlow,
Henry Denny,	Steven Smythers,
Henry Normond,	John Bland,
Jacob Roads,	Marshall Burton,
William McCollum,	Peter Warren,
Henry Denny,	John O'Harroh,
John Trotter,	Patrick Lyons,
George Sell,	William Steward,

John Hanson.

James Flanherty, Sergeant-Major, ought to have been included .
in the company. Lieutenant Lind will have him put in the
field and staff.

ROBERT GAMBLE,

Colonel Febiger's Regiment.   *Captain.*

CAPTAIN GAMBLE.

1 Captain,	6 shares each 78⅔,	-	-	-	$ 472
1 Lieutenant,	4	"	-	-	314⅔
4 Sergeants,	6	"	-	-	472
1 Drummer,	1⁴⁄₁₀	"	-	-	86½
3 Corporals,	3¹⁸⁄₁₀	"	-	-	259½
40 R. & File, 40		"	-	-	$3146⅔

60¹⁸⁄₁₀   4751⅓
Captain Gamble for goods,   -   -   -   17

Ballance paid,   -   -   -   - $4734⅓

Captain Gamble married Catharine, daughter of John Grattan,[12]
and lived for a time on a farm given him by his father. Here
his children were born in a house, still standing. A short time
after the conclusion of the war he removed to Staunton and em-
barked in merchandising with his brother-in-law, Robert Grattan,

[12] He was a native of Ireland, and is said to have been of the same
family as the distinguished leader of the Irish Parliament, Henry Grattan. He married in Scotland, Catharine —— and immigrated to Pennsylvania, but subsequently settled near Staunton, Virginia, and engaged
in merchandising. He had issue:

I. Catharine, married Colonel Robert Gamble.
II. Elizabeth, married Colonel Samuel Brown, of Greenbrier county.
III. Agnes, married Colonel Elijah Page and moved to Kentucky.
IV. Margaret, married Samuel Miller, proprietor of Miller's Iron
Works.
V. John, an officer of the Revolution, who died in service near Sun-
bry, Georgia.
VI. Robert, who was for a time a partner of Colonel Gamble; com-
manded a company of cavalry in the Whiskey Insurrection of
Pennsylvania; subsequently a farmer. He was the father of the
late Peachy R. Grattan, of Richmond.

under the firm name of Gamble & Grattan.   In 1787, Lieutenant-Colonel Gamble appears of record as a member of a court martial held in Staunton.   By this title, derived from a command in the militia, he was henceforth known.

About 1792 Colonel Gamble moved to Richmond, where he prospered greatly in business and became a highly influential citizen.   His residence at the corner of Third and Byrd streets, a commodious square building of brick, stuccoed, was demolished only a few years ago.   It was commenced to be built by Colonel John Harvie,[13] who lost his life in a fall caused by the breaking of a ladder which he had ascended to inspect the progress of the work.   Colonel Gamble purchasing the property, completed it.   The elevation on which it stood is still known as Gamble's Hill. The place of business of Colonel Gamble was a large building which stood at the corner of Main and Fourteenth streets.   His two sons John Grattan Gamble and Robert Gamble were associated with him in business under the firm name of Robert Gamble & Company.   After his death they continued the business.   They both served as officers in the war of 1812, and both removed to Florida in 1827, where they became prominent and influential. John Grattan Gamble was twice married.   His first wife was a Miss Duncan, and his second a daughter of Governor Christopher Greenup, of Kentucky.   Robert Gamble married a daughter of General James Breckinridge.

Of the daughters of Colonel Gamble, Agnes became the wife of Governor William H. Cabell, subsequently of the Supreme Court of Appeals of Virginia, and its president at the time of his death in 1849.   Elizabeth, the younger daughter, married the distinguished William Wirt, for a time the Attorney-General of the United States.   She was his second wife, his first wife, who lived but a short time, was Mildred, the daughter of Dr. George Gilmer, of "Pen Park," Albemarle county.   The death of Colonel Gamble was accidental.   He was of stout figure and was in the habit of riding on horseback to his place of business.

---

[13] Colonel Harvie was a member of the Virginia Conventions of 1775 and 1776; of the old Congress, 1778 and 1779; and the first Register of the Virginia Land Office, which he held at the time of his death in 1791.

On the morning of April 12, 1810, as he was thus on his way thither, reading a newspaper which he held before him, some buffalo skins were thrown into the street from the upper window of a warehouse he was passing. His horse took fright, started, and threw him on his head, producing concussion of the brain, which was almost immediately fatal.[14] He lies beneath an altar-shaped tomb of white marble in the church-yard of the venerable sanctuary St. John's. His home was the seat of an elegant hospitality, and within its walls were frequent gatherings of the veterans of the Revolution and of that brilliant coterie of intellect and refinement which so distinguished Richmond in the early decades of the century.

[14] The operation of trepanning was at once skillfully performed by an accomplished surgeon, Dr. John H. Foushee (son of Dr. William Foushee, the first mayor of the city of Richmond), who was within call, but it was unavailing to even arouse Colonel Gamble from the comatose condition which had been occasioned.

ORDERLY BOOK

OF

CAPTAIN ROBERT GAMBLE.

HEADQUARTERS LIGHT INFANTRY, [*August 21, 1779.*]

Field Officer to-morrow, Colo. Meggs[15] * * *
Picquett this Night, Major Stewart [adjutant]; to-morrow,
Maury,[16] orderly serg'ts from * * * and Meggs'
Reg't Colo. Meggs and Butler. Majors Hull[17] and Murfey[18]
will attend at Headquarters this afternoon at five o'clock to
receive their Dividend of money arising from the sales of the
Plunder taken in storming Stony Point July 15th, '79, which
they will receive with Proper Stated record. * * *

HEAD QUARTERS LIGHT INFANTRY,
Sunday, Aug't 22, '79.

Field Officer to-morrow, Colo. Butler.[19] Ditto for Picquett
this Night Maj'r Posey.[20] Adjutant to-morrow, Thompson.

[15] Colonel Return Jonathan Meigs, born Middletown, Conn., December,
1740; died at the Cherokee Agency January 28, 1823.

[16] Abraham Maury, appointed Lieutenant Tenth Virginia regiment,
October 8, 1777; received bounty lands from the State.

[17] Major (subsequently General) William Hull, born at Derby, Conn.,
June 24, 1753; died at Newton, Mass., November 29, 1825.

[18] Major Murfey. See *ante*, p. 224.

[19] Colonel Richard Butler.

[20] Thomas Posey (son of Captain John Posey, a neighbor of George
Washington, and who is said to have served in the French and Indian
war), was born on the banks of the Potomac July 9, 1750; died at Shaw-
neetown, Ill., March 19 1818; removed to Western Virginia at the age of
nineteen, and was quartermaster under General Andrew Lewis; participated in the battle of Point Pleasant October 10, 1774; in 1775 he
was one of the Committee of Correspondence of Augusta county;

Orderly Sergt's from Col. Butler and Febiger's[21] regiments.

	C.	Serg'ts.	C.
Daily g'd,	1	2	2
Orderly,		1	
	1	3	

For Guard to-morrow, Capt. Gamble.

HEAD QUARTERS LT. INFANTRY, FORT MONTGOMERY.

Monday, Aug't 23, '79.

Field officer to-morrow, Lt. Col. Fleury. Ditto for Picquett this Night, Col. Meggs. Adjutant to-morrow * * Benjamin.

was appointed captain and raised a company for the Seventh Virginia Continental regiment; aided in defeating Dunmore on Gwyn's Island; joined Washington's army at Middlebrook early in 1777; was transferred to Morgan's Rifles; led the regiment as Major in an expedition against the Indians in October, 1778; in the spring of 1779 took command of the Eleventh Virginia regiment; was soon after transferred to the command of a battalion of Colonel Febiger's regiment under Wayne; participated in the reduction of Stony Point, and was among the first to enter the works; present at the surrender of Yorktown; organized a new regiment, of which the rank of lieutenant-colonel, he took command; and served under Wayne in Georgia until the evacuation of Savannah. When surprised by the Indians under Guerister-sigo, on the night of June 23, 1782, Posey rallied and led his men to the charge, defeating the enemy with severe loss. From 1786 to 1793 he was County Lieutenant of Spotsylvania county, Va.; appointed brigadier-general February 14, 1793; settled in Kentucky; was elected State Senator; was four years Lieutenant-Governor; Major-General of Kentucky levies in 1809; United States Senator from Louisiana 1812-'13; succeeded Harrison as Governor of the Territory of Indiana March 3, 1813, and in 1816 became Agent for Indian Affairs, which post he held at the time of his death.

[21] Colonel Christian Febiger, born in Denmark in 1747; died in Philadelphia September 20, 1796. He had seen service before enlisting April 28, 1775, and at Bunker's Hill led a portion of Gerrish's regiment, of which he was adjutant, to the scene of battle in season to do good service. He served with marked ability throughout the war; accompanied Arnold to Quebec, and was made prisoner in the attack on that citadel; was conspicuous in the attack of Stony Point and at Yorktown, where he commanded the Second Virginia regiment. From 1789 until his death he was Treasurer of Pennsylvania.

Orderly Serg'ts from * * & Butler's Regt's.   Detail C. 1.
S. 1. C. 2 * * to parade at these quarters with Packs Slung
& one day's Provisions, at Five o'clock this afternoon Persizely,
the arms & ammunision to be immediately inspected & Returns
of Difisiances given that they may be suplide such Cartridges
as Can be exposed to the Sun on Blankets with care and attention.

	S.	S.	C.	P.
Daily g'd,	1	1	2	39.
Detach't,	1		1	9.
				48.

officers for Picquett to-morrow, Lt. Knox, for detachment to
parade at five o'clock, Lt. Craford.

HEAD QUARTERS LT. INFANTRY FORT MONTGOMERY

Aug't 24th '79

Field officer to-morrow Maj'r Hull, Ditto for Picquett this
night Col. Butler, adj't to-morrow Davis, ordily serg'ts from
Col. Meggs & Febiger's Reg't the guard ordered yesterday to
concidered as a standing Guard to mount Reggularly Every
Evening & come off one hour after Sun Rise

	L	S	C	P
Daily g'd	1.	2.	3.	38.
Night do.	0.	1.	1.	10
	1.	3.	4.	48.

Officer for Guard Lt.[22] Crittenton.

LIGHT INFANTRY, SANDY BEACH, GEN'L ORDER,

Aug't 25, '79.

Field officer to-morrow Maj'r Posey ; for night Picquett Col.
Fleury, adjutant To-morrow Maury. at a Cort Marshall held

---

[22] John Crittenden appointed second lieutenant Eleventh Virginia
regiment, July 21, 1777; promoted lieutenant, May 14, 1779.

the 24th Inst whereof Col. Putnam [23] was President, Lt. Smith of Col. Putnam's Regt. was try'd for upon a charge of taking several articils of Plunder from a soldier of the night of the storm of Stony Point, and was acquited of the Charge, the Gen'l approves the Sentence and orders Lt. Smith out [of] arrest & to join & do his Duty with his Regt. the Cort whereof Col. Putnam is President will set To-morrow morning at Ten o'clock for the Trial of Capt. Tolburt [24] of Col. Butler's Regt. & Lt. Mangard of Col. Putnam's Regt. on the Charge that will [be] Exhibited against them by Capt. Christey [25] & Lt. Col. Fleury Respectively for the Trial of all such as may be Brought before them, all Partyes to attend it is absolutely found necessary to Coutinue the Guard mentioned in yesterday's orders as a Standing Guard & to be Detained and meet on the Guard Parade at the usual time.

	E.	S	S.	C.	P.
Daily Gd.	1.	2.	3.	3.	48.
Night Gd.				1.	10.
	1.	2.	3.	4.	58.

HEAD QUARTERS LT. INFANTRY, FORT MONT'Y,

Aug't 28, '79.

Field Officers To-morrow Major Hull, Ditto For Picquett this Night Col. Meggs, adjutant to To-morrow Farell, ordily Serg't. For head quarters to-morrow From Col. Fibiger's & Meggs' Regts. Lt. Col. Fleury is officer for this Day Vice Col. Butler is Indisposed. the whole Corps of Light Infantry To Parade on Monday next at Troop Beating, the Guard of this Day to Take the Right of their Respective Regts & not to march of[f] the Parade till Reviewed by the Genl. the Standing Order for the Men's keeping Two Days Provisions Ready Cooked not

[23] Rufus Putnam, born at Sutton, Mass., April 9, 1738; died at Marietta, Ohio, May 4, 1824; colonel of engineers of Fifth Massachusetts; promoted brigadier-general January 7, 1783.

[24] Captain Jeremiah Talbott.

[25] John Christie, appointed captain Third Pennsylvania regiment, October 23, 1776.

heaving being attended to lately the Gen'l Desires the officer Carefully to Inspect it as no excuse will Be admitted For neglect of it. It is Expected that every officer appears on the Parade with their Espontoons agreeable to the Directions of the Inspecting Gen'l.

	C.	S.	S.	C.	P.
Daily g'd	1.	1.	3.	4.	47.

Officers for Guard To-morrow Capt. Grant and Lieut. Williams.

HEAD QUARTERS LIGHT INFANTRY FORT MONTGOMERY,

Aug't 29, '79.

Field officer to-morrow Major Stewart, Field officer for this Night Lt. Col. Fleury, adjutant to-morrow, Maury, ordily Serg'ts From Col. Putnam's & Butler's Reg'ts & Capt. from Col. Putnam's Reg't to sit as a member of the cort marshall which is to meet to-morrow at 2 o'clock.

	C.	S.	S.	C.	P.
Detale		2.	3.	4.	48.
Daily g'd					

Officers for Guard to-morrow Lt. Crittenton & McDowell.[26]

HEAD QUARTERS LIGHT INFANTRY FORT MONTGOMERY,

Aug't 30, '79.

Field officer to-morrow Major Posey. Field officer for Picquett this night Major Hull, adjutant to-morrow Thompson, ordily Serg'ts For Head Quarters From Col. Meggs' & Febiger's Reg'ts.

	C.	S.	S.	C.	P.
Daily g'd	1.	1.	3.	3.	49.

Officers for Guard to-morrow Capt. Booker[27] & Lt. Coalman.[28]

---

[26] Lieutenant John McDowell, Eighth Virginia regiment.

[27] Captain Samuel Booker, Fourth Virginia regiment.

[28] Lieutenant Jacob Coleman, Seventh Virginia regiment.

HEAD QUARTERS LT. INFANTRY, FORT MONTGOMERY,

Aug't 31, '79.

Field officer to-morrow Col. Meggs. Ditto For Picquett this night Maj'r Stewart, adjutant to-morrow Benjamin, Orderly From Putnam's & Butler's Reg'ts. A cort marshall held on the 27th of this Ult. whereof Col. Putnam was President, Capt. Talburt of Col. Butler's Reg't of Light Infantry was Tryed for Disobedience of orders & mutiney, the Cort Do Judge Capt. Talburt not Guilty of the Charges Exhibited against him & therefore Do acquit him. Gen'l Wayne Confirms the Sentence of the Cort marshall & orders Capt. Talburt out of arrest & to Return to his Duty in the said Reg't.

	C	S.	S.	C	P.
Daily g'd	1.	1.	3.	3.	49.

Officers For Guard To-morrow Capt. Montgomery and Lieut. Fox.

Regimental order Sept. 1st '79, the Col. o[b]serving that the Drums & Fifes in Stead of Improving themselves since they have Been on this Detachment have Grone a Great Deal worse Direct that Phillip Goaf Fifer in the 1st Battalion, and Wm. Armstead Drumer of Second take out the Drums & Fifes of the Reg't Every afternoon Sundays and Rainy Day[s] exsepted to Practice From hours From four to six o'clock, he also orders that one Battalion march Down to the old Field where they Commonly Parade, Practice Marching one hour & a half after Revalle where all the Drums & Fifes will attend this to Begin with the Second Battalion to-morrow morning and to Continue alturnately when the weather will Permit.

A Regimental Cort Marshall to set For the Trials of such Prisoners as shall be brought before him.

HEAD QUARTERS L'T INFANTRY, FORT MONTGOMERY,

Sept. 1st, '79.

Field officer to-morrow Col. Butler. Field Officer for Picquett this night Major Posey, adjutant to-morrow Farrell ordily Serg'ts From Col. Meggs' & Febiger's Reg'ts.

	C.	S.	S	C.	P
Detale	1.	1.	3.	2.	48.

Daily g'd

Officers For Guard To-morrow Capt. Gamble and Lt. Crafford.[29]

Regimental Order Sept. 1st '79 Light Infantry :

A Regimental Court Marshal Whereof Capt. Skelton[30] was President Capt. Glen was Tried [for] Disobedience of orders, absence at Role Call and Drunkenness & Sentenced to be Reduced to a Private, Sentence approved. John Bowling and John Malvin Tried for the Same Crime & Sentenced to Receive Fifty Lashes Each in Concideration of the Recommendation of the Cort and the Former Good Carrector they have had He is induced to Remit the Punishment for this time, at the Same Time Informing them that Should they Ever be found Guilty again they may expect Double Punishment for the Same Crime. Thos Roberts & Wm. Gibbs tried first for being about without Leave, Second for Drunkenness, & thirdly for not attending Role Call, and Further for Suspision of Stealing, the Theft not proved on Gibbs he is Sentenced to Receive fifty Lashes on his Bare Back. Approved. Thos. Roberts is found Guilty of all the Charges & sentenced to Receive for being about with[out] Leave Fifty & For Stealing one hundred Lashes, the Col. orders he shall Receive one hundred Lashes well Laid on· Alexander Drisdel Confin'd on the Same Charges, to Receive the same Punishment the whole to be put in execution this Evening. Thos. Roberts & Alex'r Drisdel to be Put under Stopages of half Pay until they Shall Pay Barritt the money the stold from him. Capt. Hambleton was tried for Card Playing, Contempt of the Services Reduced to a Private Sentinel and Receive fifteen Lashes, the Col. approved the First part of the Sentence But in Concideration of his former good Carrectur [was] induced to Remit the Corporal Punishment.

---

[29] Presumed to be Lieutenant John Crawford, of the Second Virginia regiment.

[30] Clough Skelton, appointed Captain Sixth Virginia regiment, January 13, 1778.

HEAD QUARTERS LIGHT INFANTRY,
Sept. 2nd.

Field officer to-morrow Major Hull, field officer for Piquett this night Colo. Gary, adjt. to-Morrow Murray, orderly sergt. Morrow from Putnam's and Butler's Regt.

Detail	C.	S.	S.	C.	P.
Daily g'd		1.	2.	3.	40.

Officer for Guard to-morrow Lt. Knox.

———

G. O. Head Quarters More's House   *   *

The Commander in Chief has the Pleasure to announce the following Resolutions which the honarable the Congress have Pleasure to Pass for the Benefit of the Army, the Disposition Manafested in these Resolves is a Fresh Pruff to the army that their Country Entertains a high Sense of their Merits and Sweets [*sic*] and are inclined to Confirm an honarable adaquitt compensation, the Genl. flatters himself their Respective States will Second the Generous V[o]ices of Congress and take Every Proper Measure to Gratify the reasonable Expectation of such Officers and Soldiers as are Determined to Share the Glory of Serving their Co[u]ntry and themselves throughout the War and finishing the task they have so Nobly begun, the flourishing aspect of officers in Europe and in the West indies as well as in the United States Gives us Every Person to beleave the happy Pride will Speedily Ar[r]ive.

In Congress, Augt. 16, 1779 :

Resolved that the Clothier General Estimate the value of the several articles of Soldiers' Clothing at the Prices they were respectively worth at the end of the year 1878, and forthwith transmit such estimate to the Pay-Masters of the several Regiments who shall be furnished out of the Military Chests. with money to pay the soldiers for the deficiences of clothing at the Estimated Price of every article as are fixed by the Clothier General who shall henceforward transmit the estimates before the close of every year during the war so that the soldiers be paid by the regimental pay-master according to such estimates annually and previous to their discharge when the same happens before the end of the year, for all articles of clothing allowed them by the resolution of Congress of the 6th of September, 1777, which they have not received and which are or shall be due to them after the year last mentioned.

In Congress, August 17, 1779 :

Whereas the Army of the United States of America have by their patriotism, valor and perseverance in defence of the rights and liberties of their country become entitled to the gratitude as well as the approbation of their fellow citizens,

Resolved, That it be and it is hereby recommended to the several States that have not already adopted measures for that purpose, to make such further provision for the officers and for the soldiers enlisted for the war, to them respectively belonging who shall continue in service until the establishment of peace as shall be an adequate compensation for the many dangers, losses and hardships they have suffered and been exposed to in the course of the present contest, either by granting to their officers half-pay for life, and proper rewards to their soldiers ; or in such other manner as may appear most expedient to the legislatures of the several States.

Resolved, That it be and is hereby recommend to the several States to make such provision for the widows of such of these officers and soldiers who are enlisted for the war or have died, or may die in the service as shall secure to them the sweets of that liberty for the maintainance of which their husbands nobly laid down their lives.

Resolved, August 18, 1779, That until the further order of Congress the said officers be entitled to receive for their subsistence money the sums following, to-wit : Each Colonel and Brigade Chaplain 500 dollars; every Lieutenant Colonel 400 dollars ; every Major and Regimental Surgeon 300 dollars ; every Captain 200 dollars ; and every Lieutenant, Ensign and Surgeon's Mate 100 dollars.

Resolved, That until the further order of Congress the sum of 10 dollars be paid to every non-commissioned officer and soldier monthly for their subsistence in lieu of those articles originally intended for them and not furnished.

LIGHT INFANTRY ORDERS,
September 4th, '79.

Field [officers] To-morrow Maj'r Murphy, Ditto for Picquett this night Colo. Butler, adjutant to-morrow Benjamin, Ordily Serg'ts [from] Putnam's and Butler's Reg'ts.   At a Gen'l Cort Marshall held the 30th of Aug't, whereof Col. Putnam was President, Lt. Manyard of the Massachusets Line was Tried on a Charge Exhibited against him By Lt. Col. Fleury For Disobedience of orders and want of Respect for a Field officer on Duty and hendering him from his visit of Guards, the Cort after Considering the Charges against him, the Evidence and his Defence thereof oppinion that he is guilty of the First Charge & of the latter part of the second, he havin By Detainin Lt. Col. Fleury a Prisoner all night acted contrary to the Instructions given by the Inspector Gen'l and hendered the Col. From Persueing his visiting the guards which might have Been atten[d]ed with Bad consequences, the Cort do therefore sentence Lt. Manyard to be Private[ly] Repremand[ed] For a conduct so highly Repprehen-[s]able as that which Lt. Manyard is found guilty of & which [the] Lives and safety of so many Brave & valliable officers & men were immediately concerned, the cannot consent to be [*sic*] therefore orders Lt. Manyard out of arest & to Return to his Duty in the Light Infantry.   At the same Cort Marshall Sam'l Harriss, Duncan McKenley & James Rarridon were tried for Leaving the Serg't & Giting Drunk when on Patrole & thret[en]ing to kill Serg't Lovel of Col. Putnam's Regiment.   Found Guilty By the Cort, Sam'l Harriss to Receive one hundred Lashes on his Bare Back well Laid on, James Rarridon one hundred do. & Duncan McKenley to Receive Fifty Lashes on his Bare Back well Laid on.   The Gen'l approves the sentence of the Cort & orders the Punishment to take Place to-morrow Evening at Retreat beating.   the Cort Marshall whereof Col. Putnam was President is Dissolved.

	C.	S.	S.	C.	P.
Daily gd.	–	1.	2.	2.	46.

Officer for Guard to-morrow Lt. Walker.

LIGHT INFANTRY AFTER ORDERS [*sic*],
September 6th, '79.

At a Gen'l Cort Marshal held this Day whereof Maj'r Stewart was Pre*dent, Wm, Matlock Soldier in Capt. Talburt's Company of Col. Butler's Reg't of Light Infantry, Charged with theft and escaping from the Quarter Guard, Disertion & attempting to go to the Enemy, was found Guilty of the whole of the Charges & Unanimously Sentenced to Suffer Death. When any Soldier becomes so Lost to Every Sence of Vallue & honour as to Be capable of commiting the Chrimes of which the above named Prisoner is found Guilty of, is no Longer fit [to] Exist in a Land of Liberty or to Remain a Disgrace to the Name of a Soldier. Gen'l Wayne therefore confirm[s] the Sentence passed by the Cort Marshall & the Same Wm. Matlock to Be shot to Death at Six o'clock this Evening, the whole of the Troops to assemble at that hour on the Grand Parade & attend the Execution. Col. Febiger is appointed President of the Cort Marshal vice Maj'r Stewart, which is set To-morrow at ten o'clock at the President's Quarters for the trial of Lt. Col. Fleury, Charged by Lt. Manyard first for ungentlemanlike behavior, second for abusing him Lt. Manyard with Insulting Language when on duty, all Evidence & Parties to have notice and attend, three Capts. from Each Regt. to attend as members.

LIGHT INFANTRY ORDERS,
Sept. 9th, 1779.

Field Officer To-morrow Majr. Stewart, Field Officer Picquett this night Major Murphy, adjt to-morrow Farell, Ordely Sergts. from Meggs' & Febiger's Regt.

	C	S	S	C	P
Daily gd.	1.	1.	3.	2.	49

L. I. O. NEAR FORT MONTGOMERY,
Sept. 10, '79.

Field officer To-morrow Majr. Murphy, Field officer for Picquett this Night Lt. Col. Shurman, Adjt. to-morrow Maury.

16

At a Genl. Cort Martial held the 9th of this instant whereof
Col. Febiger was President, Lt. Col. Fleury [was tried] on a
Charge Brought by Lt. Manyard for ungentleman Like behaviour & for Insulting Language when on Guard. The Cort
after [having] mateurly Considered the Charges Exhibited
against Lt. Col. Fleury & the Evidences, the Majority are of
oppinion that he is guilty of ungentlemanlike behaviour and
making use of Insulting Language to Lt. Manyard, But think
the Provocation he Receiv'd from Lt. Manyard, & having suffered arrest, Sufficient atonement for his Crime. The frequent
arrest[s] which hath Lately taken Place in a Corps that have
acquainted [sic—acquired?] so much Glory as to become not
only the admiration but the Envy of many, and upon whose
Conduct the Eyes of the World is fixed Give a sensation which
the Gen'l can much Better feel than Express, it affords matter
of Joy to our Publick Enemy & triumph to our Invidious Friends,
if any there be; therefore wishes the officers to Indeavour to
Cultivate that harminey and friendship that ought to subsist
amongst so distinguished a Corps & which Render them Respec-
table to their friends & to violate there Enemys [sic]; but should
there unfortunately be a misunderstanding among any of the
officers in futer, he wishes them to settle it amicably or find some
other mode than that of Court Martials or Less it be a very
Extraordinary Case in Deed. Genl. Wayne orders Lt. Col.
Fleury Immediately out of arrest and to take Command of his
Battalion, the Court Martial whereof Colo. Febiger was President is Disolved.

Detale	C.	S.	S.	C.	P.
Daily g'd,	1.	2.	3.	49	

L. I. O. NEW FORT MONTGOMERY,
Sept. 12th, '79.

Field officer to-morrow Col. Putnam, Ditto for Picquett this
Night Col. Febiger. Ordely Serg't From Col. Butler & Putnam's Reg'ts. the Gen'l Finds it absolutely necessary to Desire
the officers to be Particularly to Keep the Men in Cam[p] as
much as Possible. No Permit But from the Commanding offi-

cers of Regiments will be admited & that towards West Point only, and it is very unserting at what moment a movement may take Place, no Soldier, But in case of absolute necessity will be Permited to Pass In front or towards the Enimy's Lines which is necessary to be certified by an officer with the name of the Soldier so in Dulged, when he will Receive a Permit from the Light Infantry head quarters all Inhabitance Bringing any Kind of Produce to Camp to be admited in But not Return with out a Pass from the Commanding officer of the Light Corps for the time being at his order.

	C.	S.	S.	C.	P.
Daily g'd.	1.	1.	2.	2.	47.

After orders. members of a Gen'l Cort martial to Set to-morrow from the Light Infantry, Maj'r Stewart, Capt. Shelton & Champion.

G. O. WEST POINT,
Sept'r ye 12th, 1779.

The Gen'l Court marshel whereof Col. Marshell [31] is Prisident is Desolved. a Gen'l Court martial of the Line ordered to set to-morrow morning at nine o'clock at the usual Place for the trial of such Prisoners as shall Come before them whereof Col. Putnam is President, a Capt. from the Mariland Line, a Lt. Col. or Maj'r and one Capt. From the Pencilvania Line, the Garrison Light Infantry & Connecticut Line gives a Lt. Col. or Maj'r [and] 2 C'p'ts for the Court.

L. I. O. MONDAY, FORT MONTGOMERY,
Sept. 13th, '79.

Field officer to-morrow Col. Febiger, Ditto for Picquett this night Maj'r Posey, adj't to-morrow Farell, Ordily Serg'ts from Col. Meggs' & Febiger's Reg'ts.

[31] Colonel Thomas Marshall of the Third Virginia regiment, specially distinguished himself at the battle of Brandywine, where his regimen.t bore the brunt of the British assault led by Cornwallis in person ; the father of Chief Justice John Marshall ; after the Revolution removed to Kentucky, where he engaged in surveying.

A Fatigue Party from Each Regt. under Proper officers to be sent at two o'Clock this after noon to Clear the Parade on Top of the hill as marked out the 4th Inst. or last Sunday week.

	C.	S.	S.	C.	P.
Daily g'd	1.	1.	3.	3.	48.
Fatigue.		1.	1.	1.	16.

Officer for guard to-morrow Capt. Gamble & Lt. Craford, Ditto for Fatigue Lt. Coalman.

L. I. CAMP, FORT MONTGOMERY,

Sept. 14th, '79.

Field officer for to-morrow Lt. Col. Johnston,[32] Ditto for Pic-quett this Night Col. Meggs, Ordily Sergt's from Putnam's & Butler's Regt's, the whole Corps to Prarade Day after to-morrow at 8 o'Clock in the morning   *   *   themselves arms & accutrements in the most Soldierly order Possible the New Guard with their Respective Regiments.   When the Gen'l Beats on the Right will be the Signal to Strike and Pack their tents on Beating a March on the Right.   the whole will move in the Following order, Colo. Febiger by the Left and Colo. Butler by the Right, Colo. Putnam by the Right and Colo. Meggs by the Left and take Post on the Hill in the Rear of Garrison Leaven. Proper Intervill to Form front to the west-ward which will Throw Colo. Febiger & Butler to the North & Colo. Putnam & Meggs to the South, the officer will be ancerble for Every man belonging to their Respective Corps.

	C.	S.	S.	C.	P.
Detale	0.	1.	3.	2.	49.

R. O. *Sept. 14, '79.*

Serg't Griffin of Capt. Montgomery['s] Comp'y having for some misbehavour Been Reduced to a Private Sentinel By a Cort martial, the Col. thought Proper to approve it, But in Con-cideration of his Former Good Charactor and his Present Good

---

[32] This was probably Francis Johnston, of the Fifth Pennsylvania Regiment.

Dispersition is Pleased [to] Reinstate him in his former Rank as Serg't in said Comp'y & to Be obeyed accordingly. Capt. Montgomery will have this order Read at the head of his Comp'y at Retreat Beating to-morrow Evening when he will Reinstate him in form & he is still to Rank as Serg't from his first appointment. Lt. Col. Fleury will Immediately Call the man before him who fired his Gun to-day & severely Reppremand him & Inform him that nothing but his state of health Could induce the Col. Pard[on]ing his Point of Disobedience of Orders & that If he is Guilty again he shall Receive Double Punishment. he is to be Released from his Confinement.

CHRISTIAN FEBIGER, Col.

L. I. O. FORT MONTGOMERY,
Sept. 15th, '79.

Field officer to-morrow Maj'r Murphy, Ditto for Picquett this Night Col. Febiger, Agt. to-morrow Thompson.

	C.	S.	S.	C.	P.
Detale	1.	1.	3.	3.	48.

Officers for Guard to-morrow Capt. Hutson & Lt. Coleman.

R. O. Sept. 18th, 1779.

A Regimental Cort Martial to set to-morrow morning at ten o'clock for the trial of the Prisoners under the Quarter guard Capt. Gamble to preside, Lt. Coalman & Ens'n Fillips to attend as members. Officers Commanding Companies are to make out Returns of what arms, ammunition and accoutrements & Clothing are wanting in their Respective Companys, to the Col. Immediately.

CHRISTIAN FEBIGER, Col.

Sept'r 18th, 1779.

William Askins of my Comany is appointed a Corpora! and is to be obeyed & Respected as such.

RO. GAMBLE,
Capt. 1st R. L. I.

L. I. O. SATURDAY, *Sept. 18th, 1779.*

Field Officer to-morrow Col. Febiger, Ditto for Picquett this Night Maj'r Posey, adj't to-morrow, Maury.

The Gen'l Calls on the officers of this Corps to Pay the strictices & Immediate attention of the menuvering of the troops agreable to the mode & Rules Laid Down by the Barren Stewben. the officers will Carfully Exammen the State and Condision of the Arms, accutrements, ammunision and Clothing of their respective Comp's and see that Every thing be in Rediness to move at a moment's notis as it is more than Proverble that the next Post will [be] in an Inhabited Contry [and] the Eyes of Every Individual will be on the Light Infantry & those Officers & Battalions most esteemed who make the Best appearance on the Parrade. the Gen'l once more Calls the attention of every officer & Soldier to this assential Business as not a moment is to be Lost.

	C.	S.	S.	C.	P.
Detale	1.	1.	2.	2.	49.

Officers for Guard to-morrow Capt. Booker and Lt. Knox.

————

L. I. O. CAMP NEAR FORT MONTGOMERY,
Sept. ye 20th, 1779.

Field officer to-Morrow Major Murfree, Field Officers for Picquett this Night Colo. Febiger, Adj't to-Morrow Benjamin.

The Q. M. are Immediately to see each Company in his Respective Reg't are Furnished with two Good Axes. all such on the Ground unfit for Further Service to be Collected this Afternoon & be Exchanged for others. 4 Spades & Shovels will be also wanting. Each Reg't the whole to be Kept by the Q. Mr. or Q. M. Serg't who will be accountable for the whole at a moment's warning.

After Orders—the Troops to Cook two Days Provisions Immediately & hold themselves in Rediness to march at a moment's warnen, the Pack Horses to [be] kept with their Respective [Companies ?]

L. I. O. NEAR FORT MONTGOMERY,
Sept. 20th, '79.

Field Officer to-morrow Col. Megs.   Ditto for Picquett this Night Maj'r Hull, adj't To-morrow Thompson, Ordily Serg'ts from Megs's and Febiger's Reg'ts.

Extract from Gen'l Orders Sept. 20th, 1779 :

At a Gen'l Court martial whereof Col. Putnam was President Colo. Butler was Tryed on the following Charge, First, for Endeavouring to Excite the soldiers of Capt. Ashmead's[33] Company to meeting by ordering the Non-Commissioned officers Not to obey any order of his Capt. Ashmead; Secondly for treeting Capt. Ashmead in an unpresidently & onofficer like manner by Refusing him Liberty to wait on Gen. Wayne to Complain of Ill Treatment and Seek Redress & sending him under Guard from the L. Infantry Camp to west Point after having Receiv'd Colo. Stewart's[34] order to go to the Infantry & take the Command of his Capt. Ashmead's Company.   The Court are of Opinion that Colo. Butler is Not Guilty of the first charge, they do acquit him of Refusing Capt. Ashmead Liberty to wait on Gen'l Wayne to Complain of Ill treatment & Seek Redress, they are of Opinion that Colo. Butier was Not Justifyable in Sending Capt. Ashmead under Guard from the Lt. Infantry to west Point being a breach of [the] first article & Eighteenth section of the artickles of War & do Sentence him to be Repremanded by the Commanding officer of the Corps of Light Infantry.   The Commander-in-Chief approves the Sentence & Directs it to be Carried into Execution, at the same time he thinks Colo. Butler's Conduct Blamible in not Permitting Capt. Ashmead to see Gen'l Wayne unless he would Ingage to Comply with a Condision which Colo. Butler had no Right to anex, Nor was there any mode of such Condision as there was all

---

[33] Captain Jacob Ashmead, of the Second Pennsylvania regiment, appointed September 6, 1776 ; resigned May 16, 1780.

[34] Colonel Walter Stewart transferred from the Thirteenth Pennsylvania regiment to the Second Pennsylvania regiment, July 1, 1778; died at Philadelphia, July 14, 1796.

Ways Proper meends of Enforcing disipling of Capt. Ashmead
after applying to Gen'l Wayne Persistent in a Refractary beha-
vour.   to Prevent any misunderstanding in futer the Gen'l
Directs that the Nomination of all Capts. & sub'r to Releave
others of Nesisary or full Vacancies in the Light Corps while
it Remains together to be Reported to adjutant Gen'l & Receive
the approbation of the Gen'l before they be sent to take Command.   for this Purpos the officers Commanding Reg'ts of L.
Infantry' will Report to the adjutant Gen'l the Vacanceys that
hapen, who will Give Notices that Officers may be appointed
from the Line to fill them, be nominated by the officers Commanding the Reg'ts from which they are taken.   as Gen'l
Wayne Cannot Repremand Colo. Butler for any Part of his
Conduct Respecting Capt. Ashmead Without Violating his own
Judgment & feelings he orders Colo. Butler Immediately out of
arrest & to take Charge of his Command in the Light Infantry.

	C	S.	S	C	P.
Detale	o.	2.	3.	2.	48.

Officers for Guard to-morrow L't Fox and Ens'n Phillips.

L. I. O. Near Fort Montgomery,
Sept. 24th, '79.

Field Officer to-morrow Colo. Butler.   Ditto for Picquett this
Night Maj'r Posey.   Adjutant to-morrow Benjamine.

As a ship and one or two Galleys with some Boats has ap-
peared in View on the side [of] Dundebarge Point the Gen'l
Wishes Every Officer & Soldier to be attentive to hold them
Selves in Readiness for action in Case any attempt should be
made by the Enemy which is Rather more wished than Expected.

	C.	S.	S.	C.	P.
Detale	1.	1.	3.	3.	48.

Officers for guard Capt. Lawson[35] & Lt. McDowell.

[35] Benjamin Lawson, appointed Lieutenant, Third Virginia, March 3,
1778 ; promoted.

L. I. O. Fort Montgomery,
September 26th, 1779.

Field officer to-morrow.   Ditto for Picquett this Night Colo. Butler, adj't to-morrow Lt. Maury.

The Gen'l once more Calls upon the Officers & Soldiers to be Carefull to have two Day[s] Provisions all Ways by them & hold themselves in Readiness Ither for marching or Action in a moments' Warning.

C.	S.	S.	C.	P.
1.	1.	2.	3.	47.

Officer for Guard Lt. Chritenton.

L. I. O. Camp near Fort Montgomery,
Tuesday Sept. 28th, 1779.

Field Officer to-morrow Maj'r Hull.   Field Officer for Picquett this Night Lt. Col. Sill.   adj't to-morrow Benjamin.

	C.	S.	S.	C.	P.
Detale	1.	1.	3.	3.	48.

Officers for Guard to-morrow Capt. Booker, Lts. Craford & Coalman.

L. I. O. Camp near Fort Montgomery,
September the 29th, 1779.

Field Officer to-morrow Maj'r Steward.   Ditto for Picquett this Night Lt. Col. Hay.[36]   Adjutant to-morrow Farell.

The Troops are to Parade the day after to-morrow at troop beating, arms, accoutrements & ammunition in the Best order Possible with their Packs Slung & two Days Provision, Agreeable to the Standing order when the Strictices Scrutiny will be made [by] the officers into Every minucia, who will also be anserable For every Man belonging to their Respective Com-

---

[36] Samuel Hay, Lieutenant Colonel of the Tenth Pennsylvania; transferred from the Seventh Pennsylvania; wounded in the thigh at Stony Point; retired June 1, 1781; died in December, 1803.

panys. No Excuse can be admited for non-attendance, unsoldierly appearance, & in order to Remove Every Pretext for the latter, the Quarters master will Call on Mr. Thomas at twelve O'clock to Day Each for four pounds Sewing thread and four hundred needles, and Immediately Distribute them among the Companies in their Respective Regiments, the Commissary will Issue Soap and Candles to Each Reg't Except those who have Drawn out of the ordinary Course, in due proportion.

	C.	S.	S.	C.	P.
Detale	1.	3.	2.	49.

Officer for Guard to-morrow Ens'n Phillips.

R. O. *Sept. 30th, 1779.*

An Immediate Return to be made to the Colo. Egactly Speacifying the Number of affective [men] mentioning only the men Now belonging to the Corps Exclusith of those gone to the Hospital as those are soposed to be Retained wanting to Compleat, Likewise mentioning from what Regiments the Men are to be Draughted who are to Supply their Places that they may be Sent for those Barefooted are to be Returned in a Collum by themselves, it is with astonishment and Sorrow the Colo. observed that the men Insted of taking Pride in keeping them Selves Clean & neat are Daily decreasing in the very Necessary Point appearing on the Parade Durty & Slovenly with their Caps Laped & Sloughed about their Ears, he therefore Positively orders the officers whose Duty it is & whose Reputation in a Greate measure Depends on the appearance of their men to Pay the strictest attention to this Point & not suffer their men to appear to-morrow or any other time thereafter on Parade in such an on Soldierly like maner as here to fore, any man of Fealing must know how Disagreeable it is to a Commanding officer to Report orders of this Nature & hopes this will be the Last of the kind he will be under [the] necessity of Issueing. The Colo. Not being able to Precure Sine [*sic*] Shoes for the Officers that Each Officer Field & Staff

*   *   *   *   *   *   *   *   *   *   *   *

L. I. O. *Octob'r 4th, 1779.*

Field Officer Lt. Colo. Sill.   Ditto for Picquett the Col. Butler ; adjutant Lt. Maury.

C	S.	S.	P. F.
4.	4.	4.	200.

To Parade Immediately at the Turn of the Road on this side Harvie Straw Forge all the Guards in frunt to march to Smith's white house under the Command of the Officer of the Day & the Remainder of the troops to hold themselves in Readyness to march at a moment's warning.

	C	S	S	C	Pr
Detale	1.	1.	1.	1.	49.

Officers for Detachm't Captain Booker and Lieut. Coalman.

L. I. ORDERS NEAR HARVE STRAW FORGE,
Octr. 5, '79.

Field Officer to-morrow Lt. Col. Hay. Ditto for Picquett this Night, Col. Febiger. Adjutant to-morrow Lt. Thompson. The Q. Masters are Immediately to heave Vaults Dug one hundred and Fifty Y'ds in Front of the men & one hundred Y'ds in Rear for the Officers. Any Soldier Violating the Clearly disposion of the Camp will be Punished with great Severity. Frequent & Heavy Complaints having been Lodged with the Gen'l of the Depredations Committed by the Soldiers, he Calls on the Officers to exert themselves in detecting Marroditers [marauders ?] & when they Remember that this Army was Raised to Protect & not to oppress the Inhabitance, he is sure that Injuries so Repugnant to Freedom & so contrary to the Conduct of the Corps will never more be practised. The B. Q. M. will deliver to the Q. M. of Each Reg't their proportion of the axes.

	C.	S.	S.	C.	P.
Detale	o.	o.	2.	2.	35.

R. O. one sub Serg't, Corp'l & 24 Privates to parade to-morrow morning at Sun Rise as a Fatigue to Clear the Regimental Parade, the officers will Receive his Orders from the Colo.

L. I. O., *Octobr. 6th, 1779.*

Field Officer to-morrow Maj'r Steward.   Adj't to-morrow
Benjamin.   The whole Corps to Parade to morrow morning at
Seven O'Clock with their arms.   Ammunition & accoutrements
in the Best order.   This afternoon they will Improve in Furbishing up their Cloaths so as to make the best & most Soldierly
appearance possible.   The officers will be punctual as to the
point of time & be Careful that Every Soldier be present.

	C.	S.	S.	C.	P.
Detale,	1.	1.	2.	2.	33.

Officer for Guard Capt. Hudson & Ensign Phillips.

———

L. I. O. KAHINT, *Friday Octo'r 8th, 1779.*

Field Officer to-morrow Col. Putnam.   Adj't to morrow Lt.
Maury.   Orderly Serg'ts from   Colo.   Putnams & Butler's
Reg'ts for Light Infantry Head Quarters to-morrow.

S.	S.	Rank & file.
1.	1.	20.

To Parade this Evening at 5 o'clock with two Days Provisions Excusith this Day.   He will Receive his Orders from
Maj'r Posey.

	C.	S.	S.	C.	P.
Detale,	1.	1.	2.	2.	34.
Detachment,		1.	0.	0.	4.

Officers for Guard Capt. Lawson & Lt. McDowell.   Officer
for Detachment Crittenden.

———

G. O. LIGHT INFANTRY KATIAH, *Oct'r 9th, '79.*

Field Officer to-morrow Colo. Megs.   Adj't To-morrow Lt.
Thompson.   Orderly Serg'ts from Megs' & Febiger's Reg'ts.
The Officers are to be Particularly attentive to the Cloathing of

their men & See that their Arms, ammunition & accoutrements are in Proper Order. The whole Corps to Parade at Eight O'Clock on Monday Morning.

	C.	S.	S.	C.	P.
Detale,	1.	o.	2.	2.	34.

Officer for Guard Lieut. Walker.

LIGHT INFANTRY HEADQUARTERS, KATIAH,
Oct'r 11, '79.

Field officer to-morrow Colo. Febiger.   Adj't to-morrow Mr. Ballard.   Orderly Serg'ts from Meges' & Febiger Reg'ts.

	C.	S.	S.	C.	P.
Detale,	o.	1.	2.	2.	34.

Officer for Guard Lieut. Phillips.

LIGHT INFANTRY KAKEVATTE,
13th Oct'r, 1779.[37]

Frequent complaints are made to me that notwithstanding there are three Women who draw Rations in my Company—the Men Receive no benefit by Washing from them—for the future, to prevent complaints of this sort, and the more equitable distribution of the business amongst them.   Sergeant Grymes will imediately divide the Company into three Squads as may be most agreeable to them and give each woman a list of those she is obliged to wash for—who will deliver her the soap they draw and pay her the stimulated [sic] price—except when the soap is not sufficient & she is obliged to purchase—then they must make a reasonable allowance—but on no pretence whatever is she on an average to exceed two Dollars ℔ Dozen. the Woman's Just Accounts shall be punctually paid at the End of every month by the men except she chuses to wait Longer.   If any of the Women of my Company are properly convicted of refusing to comply with this reasonable Order, for the first fault her whole Rations

[37] In the autograph of Captain Gamble.

shall be stopt—& and for the second she shall be dismissed with disgrace as a useless charge & Expence to the Continent.

L. I. O. KAHIAT—*Octob'r ye 12th, 1779.*

Field Officer to-morrow Lt. Colo. Fleury, Adj't from Febiger's Reg't. Ordily Serg'ts From Putnam's & Butler's [regiments] The Broken and Extream Bad Ground heretofore Occupied By the Light Corps has prevented any manuvers Being practised By [the] Spirit Laid [down] in the Baron Stuben's Care of Military Discipline, But having Now taken a position that with a Little Trouble will admit of performing Most of the Useful manuvers, The Gen'l Desires the Field Officers to Cause the whole to Exercise in Battalions from Reville untill Seven O'clock Each morning, the New Guard with their Respective Corps, and from four O'clock in the afternoon untill Retreat Beating By Regiments, the Old Guards to fall in with their Respective Corps. The Gen'l wishes the Officers to attend at present to the manuvers Contained in   *   *   to Chap'r 14th. inclusive 2. Capts, 2 Sub's, 4 Serg'ts & 30 Rank & File to parade to-morrow morning with Every Ax & Spade in the Corps which was Collected by the Respective Q. Masters, this Evening, the Officers will receive their Orders from Gen'l Wayne. Adjutants of Each Regiment will furnish Maj'r Fishbourn with a Weekly Return of their Respective Regiments, they will be accordingly Carefull in making their Returns to account for Every man in the Corps as the Roster Must be form'd from them.

DETALE OF GUARDS

	C	S	S.	C	P.
Picquett	1.	0.	2.	2.	34.
Fatigue		1.	1.	1.	12.

L. I. O. *15th Octob'r, '79*

Field officer to-morrow Maj'r Stewart. Field Officer for Picquett this Night Lt. Col. Sill,[38] Adj't for the Day, Ballard.[39]

[38] David T. Still, Lieutenant-Colonel First Connecticut Regiment, appointed March 5, 1778.
[39] Lieutenant William Ballard, of the Virginia line, received March 7, 1782, 2,666⅔ acres of land for three years' service.

Orderly Sergt's from Meigs and Febiger's Reg'ts. The Loadable [laudable] Emmulation which Prevales Every Brigade & division in the army ought no where to be so conspicuous as this Corps which from present appearance May Very soone parade through Town & Cittys from which they have been Long Excluded and Eyes of citizens & Country would be more full upon the American Light Infantry than any other part of the army, the Gen'l Cort Doubt but Every Officer without distinction will Exert himself in Causing his more Immediately to furbish up the Arms & Cloathing in the best and neatest maner Possible, they have now & opening & Lather [*sic*] for the purpose, therefore no time or pains will be spared for the whole Corps to parade the day after to-morrow, the New Guard, with their Respective Regiments, the officers will concider themselves anserable for the Soldierly appearance of their men. The Gen'l observes many of the Soldiers who mount Guard Coming on the guard with long Beards & unpowdered & others the powder slovenly put on so therefore Desires the Brigade Maj'r not in futer to Except [*sic*] of any Such for Guard or any march without a bayonet but Immediately put them in & on fatigue or Camp Duty in Order to prevent the Loss of Bayonets or other material, the Field [Officer] will once Every day Inspect the Arms, Ammunition & accutrements of their Respective Battalions & make Camp Coullermda of all such that at present [are] without Bayonets & Furnish in the directest maner such as may Loose their Bayonets in futer for that Man who Looses so Cappital a wepion must be a very worthless & cowardly Soldier who is Determined to Ju[s]tify his Flight in the face of his Enemy for the want of the Bayonet. The Troops in futer will manuver But once a day that is from 4 O'clock till Retreat beating, the Old Guards will parade with their Respective Companies, the Camp picquett to assemble on the Grand parade Every night at Retreat Beating & Receive their Orders from the field officer of the picquett.

	C.	S.	S.	C.	P.
Detale,		2.	2.	32	

R. O. KAKIAT HIGHTS, *Oct. 17th, 1779.*

The Q. Masters is immediately to make application to Brigade Q. Master for the Deficiencys of Cartridges wanting to Com-

plete each man with his Rounds. The Commanding Officers of
Companies will Immediately Cause the Axes in their Respective
Companies to be Immediately Ground & put in the best order
possible. Each Orderly Serg't Will make out an Immediate
Return of the Cartridges wanting in There Companies.

L. I. O. KAKIAT,
Oct'r 18th, 1779.

Field Officer to-morrow Colo. Megs. Field Officer for Picquett this Night Maj'r Posey, Adj't Ballard, Orderly Serg'ts
from Colo. Megs & Febiger's Reg'ts.

All the Axes belonging to the Light Infantry are to be Immediately Corlected by the Regimental Q. M., Ground & Repaired
as Quick as Possible.

	C.	S.	S.	C.	P.
Detale	o.	o.	1.	2.	33.

R. O. LIGHT INFANTRY,
Oct. 22nd.

Gen'l Wayne has observed with Great Concern That the Vir-
ginians are the only troops in the Light Infantry that has not
procured Hair for their Caps. The Colo. is induced to Repeat
the Order for that purpose once more And Directs the Officers
to take the most speedy and Effectual means to procure that
Article, no officers to Mount Gard or go on the grand parade
Without a Cap, if he has not one of his own, he will [be] kind
a nuff to borrow

FLEURY, LT. COLO.
Commandant 1st. R. L. I.

C. O. *Oct'r 24th, 1779.*[40]

Captain Gamble is much pleas'd that notwithstanding the Soldiers had drawn two days rum yesterday, Ensgn. Phillips says
not one of his Company was drunk on the Parade—the Capt.
earnestly wishes this good conduct may continue & would fondly

[40] In the autograph of Captain Gamble.

hope it—But as the Commissary will soon have Liquor to Issue exclusive of what the Virg'a State so Generously has begun to Supply us with and as it may be most propper to draw several days at once on account of the distance, Soldiers who are accustomed to get drunk will by this means have it in their power. But the Captain is determined to suppress a practice distructive of good order & military discipline and does most peremptorily declare that the first man of his Company who he may catch Disguised with Liquor either on or off guard shall for the first offence have his Rum stop'd for two weeks both from the State & Commissary store, and be denied those privileges of recreation which a good and orderly Soldier can be occasionally indulged with—& for the Second Offence shall have added to this punishment whatever the sentence of a Court Martial may inflict without favour to any Individual.

———

L. I. O. KAKIAT, *October 23rd, 1779.*

Field officer to-morrow Maj'r Chapman, For Picquett Maj'r Posey. Adj't Ballard, Orderly Serg'ts from Megs & Febiger's Regt's. the troops to parade for Review at ten O'clock to-morrow morning, the New Guards with their Respective Regt's & the orders Respecting the two days Provisions Being all ways on hand & Ready Cooked Must be Particularly Observed. the Gen'l has notesed Some Neglect with Regard to the Caps and Cloaths of part of his Troops which Others have in the Cource of two or three days after Joining the Corps fully Complyed with, that order he therefore Must Conclude that the omission presides from inattention or want of meens, the whole Corps to hold themselves in perfect Readiness to march at a moment's warning, no Soldier to Leave Camp on pain of Immediate punishment without a permit from the Commanding Officer of the Reg't or Battalion to which he belongs & that Indulgence to be only but upon Very particular occasions, the nature of the Service, situation & Circumstances of the Corps Renders any other mode very improper. the Disorderly mode of beating the Revalee, troop & Retreat in this Corps Renders it highly necessary to fix on some Signal for the whole to beat of together, therefore in futer the taps to begin on the Right of the First Dawn of day &

17

to pass to & be answered from the left when the whole will begin the Ruffle, the same Ruffle to be observed for the troops or Retreat or any other Beats of the Drum that may be found necessary.

	C	S.	S.	C.	P.
Detale.			2.	2.	33.

R. O. *25th October '79*, KAKIAT.

Court Marshel to Set immediately for the Tryal of the Prisoners in the Quarter guard. Regimental Returns for the future to be made to the Virg'a State Store for the Liquor wich is to be Drawn for the men, for wich Purpose The Commanding officers of Companys will make Returns of their Respective Companys to the Quarter Master. The Q. M. to Digest them into a Regimental return & Singe [sign] it, after Wich it will be Singd by the Commanding officer of the Redg't & Sent by a Careful Serg't who will Draw the Liquor & Deliver it to the Orderly Serg'ts of Each Comp'y or Who Ever the Commanding officer of Each Company may appoint to the Care of the Liquor, The Commanding Officer of Each Company will see to have the Money Collected & Sent by the Serg't who is to Draw for the Redg't & will pay Particular Attention that when the Soldiers draw more than one gill of Liquor a day not to Deliver it to them only as the Commanding officer of the Company shall think proper.

T. POSEY, *Maj'r Com'd'g.*

R. O. KAKIAT, *October ye 26th, 1779.*

Serg't Grifee of Capt. Montgomery's Company be appointed Orderly Serg't of said Company Vice Serg't Arbright & is to be Respected and obeyed accordingly. the Commanding officers of Companies to Make Retturns of their Respective Companies for the Rum to be Drawn from the State Store Agreeably to the orders of yesterday. At a Court Martial whereof Capt. Gist was president, Saml Hunt of Capt. Lawson's Comp'y in the 1st Battalion Light Infantry was tryed for Insolence & Mutiny. the Court after maturely considering the Evidence find the Prisoner Guilty of the Charges exhibited against him and do sentence him to Receive Sixty Lashes. The Commanding Officer Looks upon the Charge to be Crime of the Deepest Die but it being a Crime which the Prisoner Never had before been Guilty and the Prisoner always behaving himself as a Good Soldier, & at the Intercession of a number of Officers the Commanding officer Remits the Punishment & orders the prisoner to be Released from his Confinement.

At a Court Martial whereof Capt. McClelin [41] was President, James Black [a] Soldier of Capt. Montgomery's Company of the 2nd Battalion of the First Reg't of Light Infantry Charged with Stealing a ham of Bacon, is found Guilty of the Charge Exhibited against him as a breach of Section 18th article 5th of the articles of War & do sentence him to Receive fifty Lashes on his Bare back the Commanding Officer approves the sentence & orders it to be put in Execution at Review beating. Serg't Ballance of Capt. Hudson's Comp'y is appointed, to Do. the Duty of Q. M. Serg't to the 2nd Battalion of Light Infantry and is to be Respected accordingly.

.   THOS. POSEY,
Maj'r Comdt 1st Reg't L. Infantry.

LIGHT INFANTRY, PERAMMONS, *October 31st, 1779.*

Field Officer Maj'r Hull. Ditto for Picquett Colo. Butler Adj't Lt. Ballard, Orderly Serg'ts from Megs' & Febiger' Reg'ts. Cleanliness being ever conducive to health, the Gen'l wishes the strictest attention of every officer to this particular Point. The Q. Masters will be Governed by the Orders of the 5th Inst with Respect to the Incampment which is to be Read at Retreat beating. The Whole Corps to Parade at Revally the Day after to-morrow with two days Provisions, the officers will be accountable for for Every Man Capable of Duty & will examine the arms, ammunition, Clothing, and accoutrements of their Respective Corps to-morrow Evening to the end that every man be in Readiness at a Moment's warning.

Detale	C.	S.	S.	C.	P.
Dayly g'd		1.	3.	2.	34

For G'd Lt. Walker. [42]

---

[41] Joseph McClellan, appointed Captain Ninth Pennsylvania July 15, 1776; transferred to the Second Pennsylvania, Colonel Walter Stewart; resigned June 10, 1781; died October 24, 1834.

[42] Lieutenant David Walker of the First Virginia Regiment.

L. I. O. Perammons, *1st November, 1779.*

Field Officer to-morrow Maj'r Stewart; for Picquett Maj'r Durry, Orderly Serg'ts from Megs' & Butler's Reg'ts.

	C.	S.	S.	C.	P.
Detale	1.	1.	2.	3.	33.

For G'd Capt. Booker & Lt. Crawford.

L. I. O. *November 5th, 1779.*

Field Officer to-morrow Colo. Butler, Ditto for Picquett this Night Maj'r Posey, Orderly Serg'ts from Colo. Putnam's & Butler's Reg'ts. Some late Intelligence Renders it necessary for the Corps to be Prepared to seek or meet the Enemy, the Gen'l wishes the Officers to make the Strictest Inspection to the Condition of the ammunition, arms, accoutrements & Clothing of their Respective Companies that nothing May be Wanting and Every man in Readiness to act at a moment's warning. the Commissary will Immediately Send Waggons & Bring the Rum & other Surplus from the Landing.

A Sub[altern] & 20 men to Parade at 4 o'clock this Evening as an Escort, he will Receive his orders at the Genl's quarters. The Troops will Manover from 3 till 4 o'Clock agreeable to a former order, at ten O'clock the whole troop to Parade the day after to-morrow, the Field officer will be Furnished with a copy of the manuver to be Performed. Every Officer & Soldier will be Present as No excuse will be admitted.

A gill of Rum will be Issued to Each man on Parade after manuvering is over & to None Elce.

	S.	C.	G'd.
Detale	1.	3.	33.
Daily G'd			
Detach't		4.	

L. I. O. *November ye 6th, 1779,* Perammons.

Field Officer to-morrow Colo. Butler, Ditto for Picquett this Night Colo. Simms [43] [?] Orderly Serg'ts From Megs' & Febi-

---

[43] Charles Simms, appointed Lieutenant-Colonel of the Second Virginia July 12, 1777 ; resigned December 9, 1779.

ger's Reg'ts. The Troops Will Leave of·Work & Improve this after Noon in Washing their Lining & Repairing their Cloathes And Furbishing up their Arms. the Tents are to be Struck and the Baggage Loaded up at Troop beating, the whole Will Parade for Inspection at ½ after 8 o'Clock & take their time of march at 9 o'Clock in the morning. Two Days Provisions to be Drawn & Cooked this Evening. the Old Guards will Join their Respective Reg'ts at Sunrise. Every Soldier Capable of Duty to march with the Company. The Q. Masters will Receive their Orders as Soone as the Bagage is Ready to move.

Detale	C.	S.	S.	C.	P.
Daily G'd	1.	o.	3.	2.	34.

R. ORDERS, *Nov'r ye 7th, 1779.*

The tents to be Pitched Immediately & Chimneys Fixt to them in the Best manner with all Possible Expedition, the Q. Master will Furnish a waggon Load of Straw which is to be Distributed to the Companies, a Corp'l & 6 [men] at the Colo. quarters & 1 Corp'l & 4 [men] for Camp Q. Guard. The Officers are enjoined in the strictest maner to Prevent the men from Destroying the Fencies or any thing belonging to the Inhabitance. No officer nor Soldier to be. permitted to go into the Country unless It is the Officers Waiters for whose Conduct their Masters will be answerable, without a pass from the Colo. or Maj'r.

CHRISTIAN FEBIGER,
Colo. 1st R. L. I.

The Commissary will Immediately engage all the Roots & Vegetables he can procure for the use of the Troops for which he will give Beef in barter on Such Days as he supplies them with Vegetables, he will only Issue ¾ lb. Flour p'r Ration with Full alowance of Beef Salt this being a Mode recommended by his Excellency Gen'l Washington and excepted by the Army. the officers & men will be convinced of the Impropriety of Granting permits to go in quest of Vegetables, a practice of this kind will have a tendency to forestall the Markets and prevent a Gen'l Supply. The whole Corps to parade to-morrow Morning with their arms, ammunition & accutrements in the Best order & they will Carry no Baggage but their Blankets and one Day's Provisions. the Officers will be Carefull that Every Man Capable off Duty turn out on the occasion. they very probably will be all wanting. the additional Camp Guard Dismount this Evening at Retreat.

A Gen'l Court Martial to set this afternoon at 1 o'Clock for the Trial of all Such Prisoners as may be Brought before them all parties and Evidences to have Notes & attend.

Maj'r Posey to preside, three Capts. from Each Reg't Except Colo. Putnam's who gives four Captains as members at the hour appointed they will attend at the president's quarter.

	C.	S.	S.	C.	P.
Detale.		1.	2.	3.	33.
C. M.					3.

Officer for guard Lt. Phillips.

L. I. O. ACQUACKANUNEH, *November 13th*, '79.

Field Officer to-morrow Colo. Butler, Ditto for picquett this Night Colo. Putnam. Adjutant, Lt. Hawkins.[44] Orderly Serg'ts from Putnam's & Butlers's Reg'ts.

	C.	S.	S.	C.	P.
Detale.		1.	2.	2.	31.

For guard to-morrow Lt. McDowell.

L. INFANTRY, *November 14th*, ACQUACKANUNEH.

Field Officer Colo. Febiger, Ditto for Picquett Colo. Megs, Orderly Serg'ts from Megs' & Febiger's Reg'ts. For Detachment at 4 o'Clock this afternoon Colo. Putnam & Maj'r Stewart, 6 Capts, 6 Sub's 12 Serg'ts, 12 Corp'ls. & 300 Privates with their arms, accoutrements & ammunition in the best order with their Blankets and Provisions—

	S.	S.	C.	P.
For to-morrow	1.	1.	1.	20—

to Mount as Brigade Guard in the Rear of the Brigade & to

---

[44] John Hawkins appointed Lieutenant Third Virginia regiment, September 11, 1777.

keep Constant Patroles Passing through the whole night on each Flank & Rear of the incampment. their Duty will be to take up & secure all Stranglers & Moroaders and unless they have a Pass Signed by Some Field Officer to be immediately punished with 50 lashes well laid on their bare backs. those who have passes as aforesaid are to be kept in Confinement untill the Field Officer who Signed the same Certifies whether he gave leave of Absence untill after retreat Beating & if he did not, the Culprit to receive his punishment. Capt. Van Heir will order his patrols of Horse to take up & deliver to the Off'r of the aforesaid Guard every soldier they may Meet with out of Camp, either by Day or Night that has not A proper pass to produce. The Commissary will furnish Fatt & Casks to Each Reg't for the purpose of making Soap. The Q. Master will immediately Cause the women belonging to Each Company & Batt'n to attend to this necessary Business. The Troops to manuver regularly every afternoon from 4 o'Clock till retreat beating at which time Each officer & Sold'r not on guard or other Duty will punctually attend the Field Officer or B answerable for Every Neglect of this Order. Daily Guard Capt. Lawson. For Detachment Capt. Shelton, Capt. Montgomery, Lt. Crawford, Lt. Phillips. Regimental Off' Capt. Gamble.

L. I. O. ACQUAKANONK,

Nov. 16th, 1779.

Field Officer Maj'r Stewart.   Do. for picquett Colo. Febiger. Orderly Serg'ts from Megs' & Febiger's Regt's.

At a Regimental Court martial held the 10th Instant, John B * * , Christian Williams & Rob't * * belonging to the artillery * * * * *

List of Officers on the Establishment of Eight Regiments in 1781, with Remarks.[45]

FIRST REGIMENT.

Colonel William Davies, Command at Chesterfield.
Lieutenant-Colonel Samuel Hopkins, Prisoner at Charlestown.
Major Thomas Posey, Rendezvous [at] Staunton.

Captains   Nathan Reid, Rendezvous New London.
             Thomas Thweatt, Prisoner—Not exchanged.
             John Overton, Chesterfield.
             Thomas Holt, Prisoner Charles Town.
             Archibald Denholm, Southern army.
             Nathan Terry, Prisoner Charlestown.
             Francis Minnis, Prisoner Charlestown.
             Joseph Scott, Jr., Chesterfield.
             John B. Johnston, Prisoner Charlestown.

Lieutenant Philip Sansum, Southern army.
             Thomas Browne, Prisoner Charlestown.
             Samuel Hogg, Prisoner Charlestown.
             Marks Vandewall, Prisoner Charlestown.
             David Walker, Prisoner Charlestown.
             Richard Worsham, Prisoner Charlestown.
             David Meriwether, Prisoner Charlestown.
             Ballard Smith, Southern army.
             Samuel Selden, Southern army.
             Joseph Conway, Prisoner Charlestown.
             Thomas Barfoot, Field Quartermaster, Chesterfield.
             Elisha King, Southern army.
             Philip Courtney, unknown where.

---

[45] This list of officers of Virginia regiments was also supplied by Dr. Cary B. Gamble, of Baltimore, Maryland, through Hon. Joseph Addison Waddell. The appended remarks indicate the condition or locality of the officer. Charlestown or Charles Town are obsolete modes of rendering Charleston, South Carolina.

Ensigns   William P. Quarles, Southern army.
            John Scott, New London rendezvous.
            John Harris, Chesterfield.
            John Carr, unknown where.
            —— Drew, just appointed.
            Robert Quarles.
            Jordan Harris.

SECOND REGIMENT.

Colonel Christian Febiger, Command at Philadelphia.
Lieutenant Colonel Gus. B. Wallace, Prisoner Charlestown.
Major Smith Sneed, on furlough.

Captains   Robert Higgins, just exchanged—absent.
            John Stith, Prisoner Charlestown.
            Alexander Parker, Prisoner Charlestown.
            Benjamin Taliaferro, Prisoner Charlestown.
            John Stokes, Prisoner on parole.
            Isaiah Marks, Prisoner on parole.
            Colin Cocke, Prisoner Charlestown.
            Robert Porterfield, Prisoner Charlestown.
            Francis Cowherd, Prisoner Charlestown.

Lieutenants Henry Moss, Prisoner Charlestown.
            Beverley Stubblefield, Prisoner Charlestown.
            John Jordan, Prisoner Charlestown.
            Thomas Parker, Prisoner Charlestown.
            James Mayborn, Prisoner Charlestown.
            John Crawford, Southern army.
            Peter Higgins, Southern army.
            Benjamin Lawson, Southern army.
            Thomas Miller, Southern army.
            William Eskridge, Prisoner Charlestown.
            James D. Laplane, Prisoner Charlestown.
            Peterfield Archer, Southern army.
            George Blackmore, Prisoner Charlestown.

Ensigns   John Heth, Prisoner Charlestown.
           George A. Washington, Aid to Marquis La Fayette.
           John Foster, Southern army.

THIRD REGIMENT.

Colonel George Mathews, Prisoner on parole.
Lieutenant-Colonel Richard Campbell, Southern army.
Major William Croghan, Prisoner on parole.

Captains   Will Johnston, Prisoner Charlestown.
            Nathaniel Pendleton, Aid to.General Greene.
            Thomas Edmonds, Southern army.
            John Anderson, Southern army.
            John Blackwell, Prisoner Charlestown.
            Will Bentley, Southen army.
            Robert Beale, Prisoner Charlestown.
            James Wright, Prisoner Charlestown.
            Le Roy Edwards, Prisoner Charlestown.

Lieutenants Thomas Warman, on furlough.
            Thomas Ransadall, Southern army.
            Henry Bedinger, Rendezvous Winchester.
            Tim Feely, Prisoner Charlestown.
            Beverley Roy, Prisoner Charlestown.
            Robert Livingston, Prisoner on parole.
            David Miller, Prisoner Charlestown.
            Benjamin Ashby, notice by letter.
            Reuben Long, Southern army.
            Will Stephens, Prisoner Charlestown.
            David Williams, Southern army.
            John Rooney, Prisoner Charlestown.
            Lipscomb Norvell, Prisoner Charlestown.

Ensigns   Peyton Powell, Prisoner Charlestown.
            John Eustace, Chesterfield.
            William McGuire, Southern army.
            John Giles, Southern army.
            Richard Archer, Chesterfield.

FOURTH REGIMENT.

Colonel John Nevill, Prisoner Charlestown.
Lieutenant-Colonel Richard Campbell, Southern army.
Major William Croghan, Prisoner on parole.

Captains   Samuel Finley, just exchanged—Major.
            Samuel Booker, Prisoner Charlestown.
            Abram Kirkpatrick, Chesterfield.
            Lawrence Butler, Prisoner Charlestown.
            James Curry, Prisoner Charlestown.
            Philip Mallory, Prisoner Charlestown.
            Willis Riddick, Prisoner on parole.
            James Crane, Chesterfield.
            William L. Lovely, sick—absent.

Lieutenants Reuben Fields, Fredericksburg rendezvous.
            John Wilson, Southern army.
            James Morton, Prisoner Charlestown.
            Robert Foster, New London rendezvous.
            Philip Easton, Southern army.
            James Holt, Prisoner Charlestown.
            Luke Cannon, Prisoner Charlestown.
            Albridgeton Jones, Southern army.
            Philip Huffman, killed—Southern army.
            Robert Craddock, Prisoner Charlestown.
            Willis Wilson, Prisoner on parole.
            Charles Erskine, C. M. S., Chesterfield.
            John Crute, Prisoner on parole.

Ensigns   Garvin Miller, Prisoner Charlestown.
            Robert Hays, Prisoner Charlestown.
            William Scott, unknown where.
            Archibald Campbell, Southern army.
            John Spitzgaddon, Southern army.
            Daniel Bedinger, Winchester rendezvous.

FIFTH REGIMENT.

Colonel William Russell, Prisoner on parole.
Lieutenant-Colonel Oliver Towles, Fredericksburg rendezvous.
Major John Willis, on furlough.

Captains   Henry Young, absent, just from Charlestown.
            Joseph Scott, Jr., Prisoner on parole.
            William Rogers, Prisoner on parole.
            Thomas Parker, on furlough.
            Custis Kendall, Prisoner Charlestown.
            Robert Woodson, Prisoner—exchange uncertain.
            James Culbertson, Southern army.
            Charles Snead, Prisoner on parole.
            Severn Teagle,[46] Prisoner—exchange uncertain.

Lieutenants Thomas Peyton, on furlough.
            Thomas Martin, Rendezvous, Staunton.
            Charles Stockley, on furlough.
            Nathaniel Darby, on furlough.
            Robert Breckinridge, Prisoner Charlestown.
            Matthew Clay, Southern Army.
            Thomas Coverley, on furlough.
            John Robins, sick—absent.
          / William Robertson, furlough from Colonel Towles.
            John Scarborough, exchange uncertain.

[46] Probably Teackle.

Lieutenants Benjamin Mosely, Prisoner Charlestown.
        Jonathan Smith, just exchanged, Philadelphia.
        John Steele, Prisoner Charlestown.

Ensigns   Jacob Brown, Prisoner Charlestown.
        Archelaus Perkins, Southern army.
        Zachariah Tatum, Southern army.
        Thomas Seayers,[47] just appointed.
        Andrew Hays, just appointed.
        Josiah Payne.

Colonel John Green, Southern army.
Lieutenant-Colonel Samuel Hawes, Southern army.
Major David Stephenson, Prisoner Charlestown.

Captains   John Gillison, Prisoner Charlestown.
        John Spotswood, Prisoner on parole.
        Clough Skelton, Prisoner Charlestown.
        Nathan Lamme, Absent—sick.
        James Williams, Lately with Southern army.
        Mayo Carrington, Prisoner Charlestown.
        John Fitzgerald, Prisoner Charlestown.
        John Nelson, Prisoner Charlestown.
        Thomas Hoard, Prisoner on parole.

Lieutenants Thomas Barber,[46] Prisoner Charlestown.
        John Townes, Prisoner Charlestown.
        Thomas Fox, Prisoner Charlestown.
        Joseph Blackwell, Prisoner Charlestown.
        James Hamilton, Prisoner Charlestown.
        William Evans, Southern army.

[47] In the State list, of those granted bounty lands, Sayers.
[46] In the State list, Barbee.

Lieutenants Samuel Baskerville, Prisoner Charlestown.
    Thomas Pearson, Prisoner on parole.
    John Hackley, Southern army.
    Nicholas Taliaferro, Prisoner Charlestown.
    John Robertson, Prisoner Charlestown.
    Charles Jones, Prisoner Charlestown.
    William D. O'Kelly, Prisoner Charlestown.

Ensigns William S. Smith, Prisoner Charlestown.
    Francis Smith, Southern army.
    Edmund Clarke, Prisoner Charlestown.
    John W. Ludiman,[49] Aid to General Washington.
    Robert Green, Southern army.
    Gabriel Green, gone home.
    James Green, gone home.
    James Barbour, gone home.
    Francis Gray, gone home.

SEVENTH REGIMENT.

Colonel John Gibson, Fort Pitt.
Lieutenant Colonel Samuel J. Cabell, Prisoner Charlestown.
Major Charles Pelham, Prisoner Charlestown.

Captains Robert Bell, Fort Pitt.
    Callohill Minnis, Prisoner Charlestown.
    Tarlton Payne, Prisoner Charlestown.
    Simon Morgan, Southern army.
    Simon Vance, Fort Pitt.
    Uriah Springer, Fort Pitt.
    Benjamin Biggs, Fort Pitt.
    George Barry, Fort Pitt.
    Holman Minnis, Prisoner Charlestown.
    John Harrison, Fort Pitt.

[49] In the State list, William J. Ludiman.

Lieutenants Lewis Thomas, Fort Pitt.
    Andrew Lewis, Fort Pitt.
    Lawrence Harrison, Fort Pitt.
    John Barnes, Southern army.
    Matthew Rhea, Southern army.
    David Allen, Prisoner Charlestown.
    Jacob Springer, Fort Pitt.
    Henry Dawson, Fort Pitt.
    John Beck, Fort Pitt.
    Jacob Coleman, Fort Pitt.
    Robert Rankin, Prisoner Charlestown.
    Philip Clayton, Prisoner Charlestown.

Ensigns Spencer Morgan, where unknown.
    John Mills, Fort Pitt.
    Jacob Winlock, Fort Pitt.
    Josiah Tannehill, Fort Pitt.
    William Connor, Fort Pitt.
    John Gibson, Fort Pitt.
    John Trabue.
    Henry Hughes.

EIGHTH REGIMENT.

Colonel James Wood, Com. Charlottesville.
Lieutenant Colonel Jonathan Clarke, Prisoner on parole.
Major John Poulson.

Captains Andrew Wallace, Killed King's Mountain.
    Thomas Boyer, Killed King's Mountain.
    Robert Gamble, Chesterfield.
    Thomas Buckner, Prisoner Charlestown.
    Presley Nevill, Prisoner on parole.
    Abraham Hite, Prisoner Charlestown.
    John Clarke, Prisoner Charlestown.
    William White, Prisoner Charlestown.
    Joseph Swearingen, Prisoner Charlestown.